A Special Gift

Presented to:

....

from:

....

date:

....

hugs™
for
teachers

#1 Teacher

Stories by
MARTHA MCKEE

Messages by
CARON LOVELESS

Personalized Scriptures by
LEANN WEISS

HOWARD BOOKS
A DIVISION OF SIMON & SCHUSTER
New York   London   Toronto   Sydney

HOWARD
BOOKS

Published by Howard Books, a division of Simon & Schuster
1230 Avenue of the Americas, New York, NY 10020
www.howardpublishing.com

Hugs for Teachers © 1999 by Martha McKee

Library of Congress Cataloging-in-Publication Data
McKee, Martha, 1934-
    Hugs for teachers : stories, sayings, and scriptures to encourage and inspire / stories by
    Martha McKee ; messages by Caron Loveless ; personalized scriptures by LeAnn Weiss ;
    [interior design and illustrations by Vanessa Bearden ; edited by Patty Crowley].
        p. cm.
    ISBN 1-58229-007-5; ISBN 1-4165-3338-9
    1. Teachers—Anecdotes. 2. Teaching—Religious aspects—Christianity.
  I. Loveless, Caron, 1955- . II. Weiss, LeAnn. III. Crowley, Patricia Caron,
1913- . IV. Title.
    LB1775.M317 1999
    371.102—dc21   98-48611
                                                CIP

30 29 28 27 26 25 24 23 22

HOWARD colophon is a registered trademark of Simon & Schuster, Inc.

Manufactured in the United States of America

For information regarding special discounts for bulk purchases, please contact Simon & Schuster Special Sales at 1-800-456-6798 or business@simonandschuster.com.

Paraphrased Scriptures © 2000 LeAnn Weiss, 3006 Brandywine Dr.,
Orlando, FL 32806; 407-898-4410

Messages by Caron Loveless
Interior design and illustrations by Vanessa Bearden
Edited by Patty Crowley

Our purpose at Howard Books is to:

- *Increase faith* in the hearts of growing Christians
- *Inspire holiness* in the lives of believers
- *Instill hope* in the hearts of struggling
  people everywhere

Because He's coming again!

CONTENTS

chapter one

Redeemed by Love

100 sheets • 200 pages
9³/₄ x 7½ in/24.7 x 19.0 cm
wide ruled • 09910

"Mis steffens is the best teacher ever. She alwas hellped me whinever I needed help. And she also hellped other peopl in my class. And when ever we did sumthing rang she did'nt talk ferm. She was very nise."

—Daniel, age 8

drawing by Alisa, age 9

You're a banker and an artist.
You're a sprinter and a florist.
You're an actor. You're a juggler.
You're a queen.

You're a lawyer. You're a manager.
You're a nurse, and you're a counselor.
You do more by noon
Than most have ever seen.

You're a driver and a poet.
A politician (don't you know it!)
You're a botanist, a strategist,
And a judge.

4

You're a mother and a father.
You're a runner and a tightrope walker.
You're a soldier fighting
In the war on drugs.

You're a diplomat and an acrobat.
You're a farmer. You're a friend.
You tell stories. You mend fences.
You build dreams

You're an instructor and a trainer,
A communicator and demonstrator.
You're a teacher! You're incredible!
You're supreme!

5

I make you stand firm in Christ.
I have anointed you, set my seal
of ownership on you, and put my
Spirit in your heart as a deposit,
guaranteeing what is to come. I
love to do far beyond all you ask
or dream through my power, which
is working in you—even when you
don't realize it.

Love,
Your God of Victory

2 Corinthians 1:21-22;
Ephesians 3:20

Essentially, learning means a change in your thinking, a change in your feeling, a change in your behavior. Learning means that change takes place in the mind, in the emotions, and in the will.

—Howard G. Hendricks

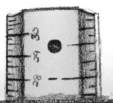

A Whole New World

"Mrs. Shearin wants you to come to her room. Hurry!" Marcy was out of breath from running when she appeared in my office door at the small private school where I was the curriculum coordinator. I quickly followed her through the library and down the elementary hall to Mrs. Shearin's second-grade room. Marcy opened the door, and we stepped into a classroom frozen in awe.

Nine students stood motionless behind their desks facing the reading table in the back corner. No one moved or looked in our direction as we softly closed the door. A child's voice smoothly intoning sentence after sentence—never missing a word—was the only sound in the room. The other children, still seated at the reading table, were no longer looking at their books but were watching in amazement as their classmate read the text flawlessly. Mrs. Shearin glanced at me with an astonished expression, nodded toward the reader, and turned her attention quickly back to her manual.

The reader was Allen, a child who entered our school after having attended five other schools in the previous two years. His records showed excessive absences, poor academic progress, and frequent discipline problems. His mother had pleaded for his admittance, citing his needs to be in a stable atmosphere and to make friends who were interested in learning. After promising to cooperate with the staff during his adjustment period and making a commitment to his regular attendance, his mother's request was granted.

The first few weeks were difficult. Sheri Shearin was known as a consistent, loving but firm disciplinarian whose goal was restoring children to pro-

ductive learning. Allen stretched all of these quali-
ties to the extreme. In the beginning, he would
sometimes get so frustrated with schoolwork that
he blurted out words that would normally evoke a
swift and severe reprimand. But instead, Sheri
would call him to her desk, put her arm around
him and say, "Those words are just not tolerated in
this school. When you don't know what to do, raise
your hand and I'll help you. Now, tell me what you
are going to do the next time you feel like that."
After he rehearsed the correct procedure, Sheri
would assure him that she loved him and believed
in his ability to do the right thing. The rest of the
class would listen to the softly spoken exchange
with rapt attention, knowing that they would never
get off that easy. On his third day, he punched a
third grader in the stomach at recess, and his
absence for the remainder of the school day was
greeted with sighs of relief.

Sheri knew that she could not effect lasting
changes in Allen without the understanding and
cooperation of his classmates. She also knew that if
they could accept him, honor his good points, and

love him in spite of his difficult behavior, they would benefit even more than Allen.

Negotiating a fine line between giving Allen the attention he needed and breeding jealousy in the other students, Sheri made time for celebrating the uniqueness and individual successes of each child in the class, and the students responded with new levels of appreciation for each other. She worked hard to orchestrate chances for Allen to be successful in the eyes of the other students. She used Bible stories to teach forgiveness and compassion. She created an atmosphere in which Allen felt accepted—even when he returned from one of his frequent trips to the principal for infractions committed outside the classroom. Students who grumbled at his inattention and slow responses were quietly encouraged to be patient and helpful. Parents who asked about the new boy or volunteered in the room were drawn into the loving-socialization-of-Allen process. Sheri molded her class into a loving community every way she knew how.

Allen had just as much trouble academically as he did socially. He struggled with simple addition problems, his spelling was atrocious, and understanding the concepts of social studies was almost beyond his grasp. Including Allen in whole-group learning slowed the class down so much that sighs of impatience were regularly heard from the other students. Whenever he was asked to give an answer, everyone had to wait for him to be shown the page the class was on. But nothing seemed to frustrate Allen more than his difficulty with reading. When his turn came in the reading circle, he would stammer and stutter and his face would turn red as he struggled with all his might to make out the words. Of all the things he failed at, it seemed that he wanted to succeed at reading most of all.

And now, Marcy and I stood dumbfounded as we listened to Allen reading flawlessly from his second-grade reader. He was enraptured by the story of a little boy who had a new pair of moccasins. Maybe he felt an affinity for the boy in the story. Maybe his intense desire to read brought all his skills into focus. Maybe the love and acceptance of his teacher and classmates had finally translated into enough self-esteem for him to believe that he could read just as well as his classmates. Whatever the reason, the moment was magic—to Allen, to Mrs. Shearin, to his classmates, and to me.

Allen finished the story and turned to look at Mrs. Shearin, who had tears streaming down her smiling cheeks. She threw her arms around him in a hug of celebration. That is when the applause began.

I'd never seen anything like it before, and I've never seen anything like it since. All Allen's classmates were applauding, and one by one, the remaining seated students rose to their feet to give him a unanimous standing ovation. When his teacher released him, Allen stood beside his chair and bowed deeply—something he had seen a soloist do at a musical performance just last week. That was when the cheering began.

Allowing the noise to die away naturally, Sheri joined me at the front of the room to watch, as each student congratulated Allen. One of the best readers in the class told him, "I want to read that story again. You made it sound better than when I read it myself."

That day was a watershed for Allen. With his confidence soaring, his reading skills developed rapidly. His self-control and social skills improved steadily, in spite of occasional lapses. He gained a whole year on his skills tests during the second semester alone.

Mrs. Shearin's students experienced firsthand the transforming power of kindness and compassion, and one more child stepped out of confinement and into a whole new world of possibilities.

Lord, let me be a
Conduit of love and confidence
To children who have known nothing but defeat.
Use me to help each child uncover
The gifts you have placed within.

Recess

Sit back, take a deep breath, and meditate on ways you can inspire character in your students . . .

chapter two

Restored by Grace

100 sheets • 200 pages
9³/₄ x 7¹/₂ in/24.7 x 19.0 cm
wide ruled • 09910

"Mrs. Bennett was the bestest teacher I had. She was fun, sweet, and nice. I once gave her some chocolate and she ate it."

—Ginnie, age 8

drawing by Cole, age 7

It's been said the best teachers are lifelong learners. An even better motto may be that the best teachers learn some of life's greatest lessons from their own students.

Students are chock-full of valuable information. They keep you in tune with the hottest music. Their wardrobe exposes you to the latest fashions. Their slang adds color and variety to your vocabulary. Even their New-Age views force you to pull out and polish up the sacred origins of your own cherished beliefs. But, probably, the most valuable lessons of all come from those students who teach you about yourself.

Let's face it. Some students can get to you, and certain classes have a way of dredging up some pretty stinky attitudes. They tromp around in the muck of your soul and steal the joy from your job. Just moments in the presence of some pupils, and the patience is sucked right out of you.

You scowl and threaten and pull your last hair. It's here, when the tables of teaching have overturned, that God will most likely show up. He'll have a word for you. He won't be angry. More, than anyone else, he understands about unruly, undisciplined disciples. But his word for you will get to the heart of the matter and go something like this: When a student hands out a "test," a smart teacher will take the time to grade her own paper.

Maybe the greatest teachers of all are the ones who learn to see their most challenging students as tutors from heaven instead of terrors from hell.

Make the most of every opportunity, because the days are evil. Be wise. Don't be pressed into reacting like the majority of the world. Instead, rise above the circumstances and see yourself transformed by renewing your mind with my higher principles. Use the special gifts and abilities I've given you to serve others; faithfully administer my amazing grace as only you can.

Love,
Your God of Incomparable
Riches of Grace

Ephesians 5:15–16;
Romans 12:2; 1 Peter 4:10

Every good teacher is a student of students. After all, if he is to venture to cross over to the student's side of experience, he should have some idea of where he is going, and how to get there.

—Wayne R. Rood

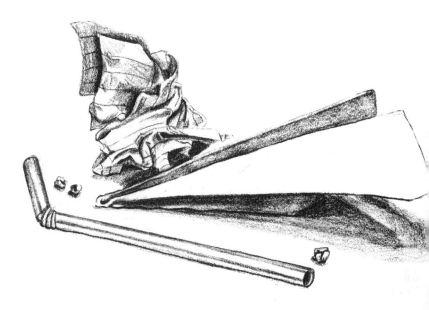

I Know Him Too!

Everyone knew Jeb. On the first day of the year, he told the school secretary that he didn't want to be in this school. Three giggly sophomore girls who approached him at lunch that day were greeted with an angry glare before he turned his back on them, stuffed his sandwich into his pocket, and walked sullenly away. Many students tried to befriend him, but to no avail. At first, when teachers pressed for responses in class, he spoke in a barely audible voice, but recently

Jeb had begun to complain loudly that even routine assignments were unreasonable.

During lunch on Thursday, Jeb's annoying new behavior pattern was the main topic of discussion. Mr. Conner had seen no signs of the complaining in his class, but he finished his sandwich, quickly reviewed Jeb's records, and prayed.

Everyone knew Mr. Conner. He taught English and coached baseball. Mr. Conner was physically powerful but gentle and caring with his students. He made no secret of his love for Jesus.

On Monday Jeb was having a "worse than usual" day. Before lunchtime, two of his teachers had already sent him to the vice principal's office when his complaining progressed from disruptive to disrespectful. He was given detention and a stern warning.

Mr. Conner began fifth-period class by announcing, "Today you will begin a rough draft of your essays. We have analyzed several examples of essay writing—some were really good, and some were not so good." As he distributed stacks of papers to the first person in each row, he explained, "We have discussed eight guidelines for writing effective essays, and I have listed them on this sheet. Stay focused..."

"You mean you want us to do all this—everything on this sheet?" Jeb interrupted, waving his copy of the paper in the air.

"Yes," Mr. Conner answered with a smile.

"Jeee - susss!" Jeb swore as he slammed his notebook shut, sending it and his book crashing to the floor.

The other students held their breath as they turned in unison from the angry Jeb, anticipating Mr. Conner's outraged response.

Mr. Conner didn't look outraged.

Jeb's eyes narrowed as he waited for another confrontation like the two he had precipitated that morning with his history and algebra teachers.

With a hint of a smile, Mr. Conner gently closed his plan book, placed it softly on the lectern, slid his hands into the pockets of his slacks—making his biceps and shoulders look massive—walked slowly toward Jeb's desk, bent down inches from his face, locked Jeb's eyes in a close-up gaze, and in a tone of absolute love and wonder, said, "I know him too!"

Restored by Grace

The whole class exhaled as they saw all the color leave Jeb's face.

"Yes sir," was all he could whisper.

"Give the assignment a try, Jeb. I'll be right here if you need me."

Jeb picked up his notebook and pencil.

That Monday the English class saw Jesus.

Jesus, Master Teacher,
Help me see beyond destructive behavior,
Beyond the icy glares and slamming books.
Give me your insight and your grace,
So they may see you reflected in my eyes.

Recess

Relax and contemplate how you can represent Jesus to your students . . .

32

chapter three

Remembered by a Child

100 sheets • 200 pages
9³/₄ x 7¹/₂ in/24.7 x 19.0 cm
wide ruled • 09910

"My favorite teacher is Mrs. Calloway. She is sooo nice! She has poofy hair and wasn't like a teacher. She was like an ordanary person. She was funny, loving, caring, and always had something nice to say."

—Erin, age 10

drawing by
Annabeth, age 6

ith a mind like yours, you could
have landed almost any kind of job you
wanted. The field was wide open. Your
options seemed endless. But at the end of the
day, you counted the cost, assessed your talents, and set your feet on the path of your heart.
Even now, even on the hardest days, you're
still glad you traveled down this road. You've chosen a career that embraces the lives of children,
and if you stop to think about it, you're in
mighty good company. The Savior of the world
was also a teacher. In fact, when it was all said
and done, he did more teaching while he was
here than anything else. And just like you,
he had a soft spot for children.

Jesus got down on their level and
related to children as a friend. He
spoke their language, defended
their innocence, and gathered
them up in his arms. His
disciples   complained

Tuesday### Inspirational Message

that children were a waste of
time. After all, what did they have to
offer? But also like you, Jesus knew better.
He recognized the vast potential in each of
those young lives. And when he looked into
their eyes, what he saw must have spun his soul
into orbit, for there in abundance was the qual-
ity that pleases God more than anything else.
Faith.

As you journey down the path of teaching,
take heart in the fact that Jesus Christ, the
Teacher, has walked there before you, leaving
his own large footprints as a guide. And go
with the joy of knowing that he has
graced with his glory the profession
that you've chosen.

Your students can't see me directly. But if you love them, I live in you and my love is made complete in you. Pass my love on with action and in truth. Whoever welcomes a child in my name, welcomes me.

My everlasting love,
God

1 John 4:12;
1 John 3:18; Matthew 18:5

Abruptly, circumstances arrange themselves so that the commonplace becomes the significant and the routine memorable. . . . Afterward you know that you have learned something valuable—something that can't always be described exactly, or measured, or fully explained. But something.

—Arthur Gordon

In a Child's Eyes

There I was again, trying to do the grocery shopping on the way home from school. Searching for fresh apples in the fruit bins at Safeway, I felt someone at my left elbow. Glancing down, I saw a small child staring intently at me. I waited for him to speak, but he just stared.

Finally, I smiled. His wide eyes never blinked, but his jaw dropped slightly. He stood transfixed.

"Hi," I said.

No response.

Finally, he turned and ran down a nearby aisle. Strange!

I moved on to the onions and lettuce, still trying to disengage my mind from the day's classroom events before I got home. Later, pushing my cart toward the meat counter, I came alongside a young woman whose son was pulling at her sleeve, pointing in my direction, and shouting, "But, Mama, that's her! That's her! She's the lady who saved my life!"

Why hadn't I recognized him?

Yesterday, as I stepped out of my classroom to take a report to the office, I met a teacher walking down the hall and holding this little boy's hand. He was clutching his throat with the other hand, and his eyes were wide as saucers. They were also walking toward the office.

"He has a ball of hard candy stuck in his throat," she explained in a tone of disgust. "He knew he wasn't supposed to have the candy in his mouth when he was on the monkey bars. He knew better." They had obviously walked all the way in from the playground. The child should have already passed out; I couldn't believe that she didn't realize the danger he was in. We were still a long way from the office, and she was expecting him to walk the remaining distance with no more assistance than a held hand.

Huge, desperate eyes pleaded for help.

Without thought, I dropped my report, picked him up by the waist, and dropped his head down. Almost immediately, the candy popped against the tile floor and rolled down the hall. I put him on his feet and knelt to see if he was all right. "Is your throat clear now?" I asked.

He took one cautious breath then three deep gulps of air and nodded yes. Suddenly, he threw his arms around my neck and hugged hard but said nothing. I hugged him back and met his sober-faced gaze for an instant.

His teacher retrieved the candy ball with a tissue and stepped through her classroom door to drop it in the trash basket. The boy followed her but turned in the doorway and stood staring at me.

Today that same little boy was standing in front of the meat counter in Safeway announcing to every customer within earshot that I had saved his life.

Remembered by a Child

His mother was embarrassed at what seemed to be an obvious overstatement of truth and the stares her son was attracting. Trying to hush the commotion, she mumbled, "Please, John, be quiet!" She gave me a bewildered glance as she pushed her cart and John toward the front of the store. I saw him look back at me just before they disappeared around the corner.

I wanted to stop her and tell her that her son had been in danger, but I couldn't figure out how to validate his words without appearing to be interested in validating my own heroism. I had done nothing more than thousands of teachers do every day without thinking. Unable to find the appropriate words, I said nothing.

Later, I saw John come to the end of the cereal aisle and stare at me again. This time I whispered, "I'm glad you're okay." This time he smiled.

Standing there, holding my grocery list but savoring the hug he gave me yesterday and the smile he gave me today, I realized that John had been far more frightened and far more grateful than I could ever imagine. How, I wondered, could an event that was only a momentary pause in my eyes have been such a momentous occasion in John's eyes? I guess it is a matter of perspective.

Good teachers perform miscellaneous acts of kindness every day without a second thought. But in the eyes of a child, the smallest gesture may be heroic indeed.

Give me, Father,
The eyes of a child.
Teach me to see each simple kindness
As a genuine act of heroism.

Recess

Use this quiet time to reflect on the power of your influence for good . . .

_____

_____

_____

_____

_____

_____

_____

_____

_____

_____

_____

49

chapter four

Relieved by the Truth

100 sheets • 200 pages
9³/₄ x 7¹/₂ in/24.7 x 19.0 cm
wide ruled • 09910

Miss Joy is a graet Sunday school teacher. I like Miss Joy becase she gives stickers to the people who are quiet. She is graet. And she loves me.

—Caleb, age 8

drawing by Ashley, age 9

$\mathcal{M}$uch of your life has been focused on grades. First, there were grades you had to make to please your parents. Then came grades you had to get to enter college. And now, it's grades that you must give to all your students.

In fact, grades have probably become such a priority that if you were asked the question, "If your house was on fire and you could take out only one book . . ." no doubt you'd say, "My grade book!"

Grades are helpful—they're important measuring tools. Grades are motivating—they often spur achievers on to greatness. But after being in an atmosphere of evaluation for a long time, you might begin to compare yourself to others—and that can spell trouble. Some things just weren't designed to be graded . . .

Can you grade a glowing sunset
Or flashing bugs inside a jar?
Can you rate a velvet rose
Or score the sparkle of a star?

Dare you judge between a dewdrop
And the swells that storm at sea?
Can you gauge a gliding swan
Or appraise the sweetness of a peach?

What's the measure of a mountain?
What's the rank of rabbit's skin?
What's the status of a fountain?
Try to grade a baby's grin.

When you were born, God didn't give you a grade; rather, he announced his opinion of you to the whole world. And it was . . . *very good!*

His love for you is not determined by your performance. Practice agreeing with what the God of the universe says about you. And work at keeping the grades where they belong: in your grade book.

The fear of my Father is the beginning of wisdom, and knowledge of the Holy One is understanding. Hold to my teaching and you will know the truth. My truth will set you free.

Love,

Jesus

Proverbs 9:10;
John 8:31-32

The whole art of teaching is only
the art of awakening the natural
curiosity of young minds for the
purpose of satisfying it afterwards.
—Anatole France

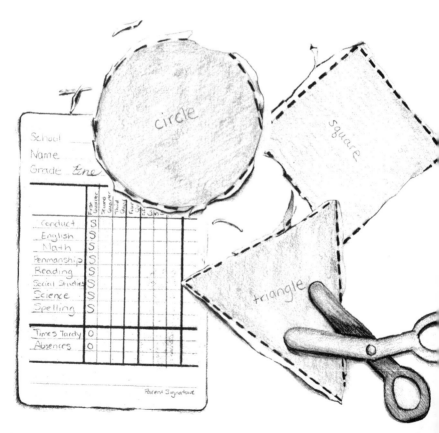

First Report Card

Cody had wanted to go to school all his life. His dad, a high-school coach, was working on his law degree during the off-season. His mother, a teacher, was always reading on some new subject she wanted to know more about. His older brother, Matt, was in fifth grade and had learned about some amazing places in the world. Cody could hardly wait to go to school.

Finally, he was really there, in his own desk in first grade. His teacher was nice, and

Cody was able to do all the papers she gave him without any trouble.

By the end of the first six weeks of school, Cody was bringing home picture books and "reading" them to his mom. He knew he wasn't the worst reader in class, and he suspected he might be one of the best.

Then came report-card day. Cody had watched the report-card routine with his parents and Matt for years. They always looked for A's, and once when Matt got something besides an A, he was grounded. Cody was pretty confident that he'd get all A's. He had worked hard, and his teacher had bragged on him. His parents would be proud!

When his teacher explained how the report cards would look and their purpose, Cody was looking out the window thinking, *A's! I'm not going to get anything but A's as long as I'm in school. A's are like winning the football game. I'm really going to be good at this school thing.*

The teacher called his name. He shouldered his backpack and walked proudly to the door where she gave him his very first report card and an encouraging hug. Matt was going home with a friend that day, and Cody was to walk the few blocks home alone. He made his way through the crowd in the schoolyard before he pulled the card from its envelope and looked. He couldn't believe it! He had flunked first grade! He shoved the card into his backpack and turned toward home. But when he got to the creek, he stepped off the sidewalk and slid down the steep bank to his secret place under the bridge.

He pulled the card out again and studied it hard while the buses and cars rumbled over his head. He was right: not a single A in the whole column. What could he do? What would his parents do? He couldn't bear to think of their disappointment. He'd just sit here all night.

He had no idea that he had been missed almost immediately or that Matt had been called home to look for him. He had no idea that he had been under the bridge only forty-five minutes; it felt like hours. He did know that he was really hungry.

Scrambling up beside the bridge, dragging his backpack, Cody was glad to be heading home. If they grounded him for the rest of the year, home was better than a muddy creek bank—and if he remembered correctly, Matt still got to eat while he was grounded. He had scarcely walked a block when his brother spotted him. Matt ran to meet him, grabbed his hand, and raced toward home with Cody's backpack flying along behind.

"Mom, I've got him!" Matt yelled as he jerked open the back door.

Along with all the hugs and tears came the questions, "Are you hurt?" "Where were you?" "Were you alone?" "Why were you under the bridge?"

He looked around the room at the worried faces. Even Mrs. George from next door was there. He didn't want to tell about his failure with everyone listening, so he whispered to his mother, "I got a bad report card. Shhh! I don't want *her* to know." His nod indicated the visiting neighbor.

His mom got the message. She thanked the neighbor and ushered her out the back door just as his dad rushed in from the fieldhouse asking all the questions again. "Is he hurt?" "Where was he?" "Cody, why were you under the bridge?"

"He said something about a bad report card. Do you want to show it to us now?" his mom asked.

First Report Card

Cody pulled the smudged envelope from his backpack. He slid the card out and laid it softly on the table. Four heads bent close. "I can't read all that," he said as his hand swept over the skill explanations in the first column, "but I know those are not A's, they're S's, and S's are way down the alphabet! I guess I just flunked first grade."

His parents and brother burst out laughing. Matt was the first one able to speak. "You're right, Cody, they are S's. They stand for *satisfactory*. That's the best you can get in first grade! It means you're doing real good. In higher grades, you'll get A's and B's—but you'd better not get a C, or you'll get grounded."

That night at the football game, Cody asked his friend Tommy, also a first grader, "What did you get on your report card today?"

"I got all S's!"

"Me too!"

They slapped a high-five and raced over to swing on the railing.

Relieved by the Truth

Gracious Father, give me ever eyes of grace.
Though I must evaluate and assess,
Help me always see the special talents of
Each and every child.
Teach me how to show my students the
Beauty of your image in their souls.

Recess

Quiet your heart and thank God for his mercy and grace . . .

_____

_____

_____

_____

_____

_____

_____

_____

_____

_____

_____

5

chapter five

Rescued by Compassion

100 sheets • 200 pages
9³/₄ x 7¹/₂ in/24.7 x 19.0 cm
wide ruled • 09910

69

"My teacher is sweet.
And she loves frogs.
We call her the
froglady. And she is
the one that I love
best. She allso looks
like my grandmother."

—Raymond, age 9

drawing by Brittany, age 9

$\mathcal{I}$t doesn't stop here, you know. Like dandelion seeds strewn across a meadow, what you do just keeps on going. God takes your acts of love, those wispy, wiry pods, and launches them out with the gust of his breath. The deeds of your hands are sprinkled here and there throughout the land, escorted by the winds of his Spirit. No. It doesn't stop here. It multiplies.

Like rippling rings on a pond, your encouraging words, your positive reinforcements, and your assuring smiles are all going places. Places that thirst for these things, places you could never go yourself, into lives you'll never get to meet.

But really, you want it this way. It's the way it was for you. You yourself are a ring from someone else's splashing rock. Like branches of shade, your effort doesn't stop here. It goes on to

72

cool other souls. Like you, it will
reach out, comfort, shelter, and accept.

None of it stops with you. It started
with you, but it won't stop there. Not by a
long shot.

Your students are the vehicles. Some will be
teachers themselves.

They will carry your gifts away. Your kind
words, your pure passions, and your guiding
light will be passed out by them like bread to
the hungry. They will take your humble light
and set off diamonds in the sky. There will
be fireworks in the future. People will gasp
at their dazzling display, delight in their
shimmering brilliance—all ablaze from
your one tiny spark.

Oh no, dear teacher. It doesn't
stop here.

I've started a good work in you. When you feel overwhelmed and at the end of your rope, look up and remember that your help comes from me! Please don't lose heart in doing good, for in my perfect timing I promise you'll see a reward if you don't give up. Be confident that I will faithfully complete the things I've birthed in you.

Love,
Your God of Redemption

Psalm 121:1-2;
Galatians 6:9; Philippians 1:6

A teacher affects eternity; he can
never tell where his influence stops.
—Henry Adams

It's a
Wonder

His students knew he wasn't like the other teachers. Word gets around in a high school, and word had it that his Distributive Education class was "real." He related to teens on their own level, and the class was practical and fun. If you were straight with him, you could trust him with your life.

The wonder was that he became a teacher at all.

Buddy was the youngest of four children. His mother barely survived his birth, and her recovery was slow. His twelve- and fourteen-year-old sisters cared for their mother, who had sunk into depression, as well as Buddy and their two-year-old brother, who was still in diapers. Their father stopped by his crib occasionally to curse the additional mouth to feed.

By the time he was six, his two sisters had graduated from high school and were no longer living at home. His brother was adopting their father's pattern of emotional and physical abuse, and Buddy was easy prey. But that fall he went to first grade.

School was the most wonderful place he had ever been. There were lots of children his own age to play with, and most of them were nice to him. Best of all, his teacher hugged him every day and told him how smart he was. Although he tried to do everything she said, there were so many exciting things to see and so many new friends to talk with that he just couldn't concentrate on reading. Besides, his family didn't act like Dick and Jane.

Second grade was even better. He had learned that he could make people laugh, and every lesson contained at least one idea for a joke. His teacher enjoyed his sense of humor and was sure that reading was not out of reach for such a bright little mind.

Third grade was a different story. That year his teacher expected her students to produce work on grade level and had no patience with students who couldn't. Early in the year, Buddy came to school without his homework. The tension and conflict had been especially bad at home the night before, and he didn't even know where his paper was. Mrs. Smith called him to the front of the room, paddled the palms of both his hands, pulled his desk into the closet, put another paper in front of him, and closed the door. He was crushed. School had always been his refuge. Now he had to defend himself here too.

He spent fourth through twelfth grades perfecting the art of "getting by." His complex diversionary tactics required extraordinary creative thinking and analytical skills. At graduation, his teachers shook their heads and wondered how someone so obviously bright could graduate after having done so little.

Not until after a four-year stint in the navy did he realize the importance of an education, and he determined to enter college. His English teacher, Mrs. Stapleton, handed him a copy of *Kon-Tiki* and said, "To be successful in college, you will need to read well and write well. There will be an essay test on this book next time the class meets. Be prepared to discuss it when you come in the door." That week Buddy read an entire book for the first time in his life. Loving, encouraging, and tough, Mrs. Stapleton pushed him into working hard then bragged on his progress. None of his old diversionary tactics worked with her, and for that she earned his deepest respect. His love for learning was redeemed.

Who would have thought that this little boy from an unhappy home would became a teacher and school administrator himself?

And so, equipped by all the loving, creative teachers who had invested in his life, Buddy stepped into the tense silence of a first-period shop class. This was not the first time he had been summoned to help a teacher deal with a potentially explosive situation. The weary teacher sat stiffly behind his desk, hands on his knees.

It's a Wonder

Buddy's tone was friendly and casual as he addressed the disruptive student. "Have a seat, Joe, and we'll start class." Joe didn't move. As vocational administrator, Buddy knew all the students sitting motionless in their desks, eyes fixed on him.

"You know the procedure, Joe," Buddy said. "Either sit down so we can start the class according to state guidelines or meet me in the vice principal's office."

Joe moved toward the door, slowly at first, then running. "I don't care how hard you hit me, it can't be as bad as what I got at home last ni..." His last word was lost in the slam of the classroom door.

When Buddy walked into the office, Joe was already sitting with his head in his hands. Buddy touched him lightly on the shoulder and said, "Come on, Joe, we have business somewhere else." That Friday and every Friday morning until school was out, Joe and Buddy had breakfast together during first-period class. Over biscuits and gravy, Joe vented his frustrations, and Buddy helped a troubled boy reshape his life.

Rescued by Compassion

Lord Jesus,
Help me recall my own childhood memories—
Both good and bad—
And use both to be a better teacher.
Remind me to see the child I'm teaching
And not just the papers he turns in.
Remind me to be like you.

Recess

Take a breather and assess your goals as teacher . . .

_____

_____

_____

_____

_____

_____

_____

_____

_____

_____

85

chapter six

Refreshed by Success

100 sheets • 200 pages
9³/₄ x 7¹/₂ in/24.7 x 19.0 cm
wide ruled • 09910

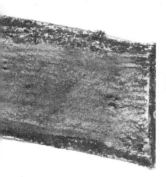

"My favorite teacher is Mrs. Jolles becaus she is very strict. If she wasn't i would probly have no maners or anything like that. And she teaches me other work."

—Jon, age 10

drawing by Zachary, age 10

$\mathcal{A}$mong all your former teachers, who is the one that to this day inspires you? Who first challenged you to "think outside the box"?

Who took special interest in your work? Who motivated you to get to class early, stay up late, or dream bigger dreams? Which one of your teachers or professors awakened you to a subject that had a previous history of putting you to sleep? Which teacher stoked your courage to give a speech, try out for a play, or apply for a coveted scholarship? Of all of them, who was it you lived to please most?

Why not stop for a moment and visit that teacher again? Recall the wonder you felt in her presence. Think about the new direction you pursued as a result of his comments or her advice. Imagine what you would have missed had that teacher not been assigned to you.

Believe it or not, this week some student is looking up at you with the same sense of awe you felt for your teacher. Somewhere amidst the sea of often blank faces, a student is leaning in to catch your every word. He is listening. She is getting it. Thanks to you.

Let the honor sink in. Let the thought of it invigorate your lessons. Celebrate the fact that long after you're gone, your name and today's investment will be alive and thriving in someone's soul. One day, you may see these students again, hear of their achievements, and feel it was worth all the effort. Until then, bask in the knowledge that every time you teach, you invest in your own living legacy.

I am for you! Watch me multiply your efforts. Because of my power working in you, the outcome is far beyond all that you can ask or dream. Nothing is too difficult for me.

Faithfully,
Your God of Victory

Romans 8:31;
Ephesians 3:20; Jeremiah 32:17

In teaching you cannot see the fruit of a day's work. It is invisible and remains so, maybe for twenty years.

—Jacques Barzun

Hidden Potential

The door key refused to go into the lock, overloaded grocery bags threatened to spill, and the phone rang persistently inside. These transition moments from teacher to wife and mom always stressed me. The pleasures and frustrations of a day in the classroom begged to be savored or resolved, but family activities and responsibilities pressed in.

Finally, the door swung open, and I reached for the ringing phone as my bags dropped onto the kitchen table.

Refreshed by Success

"Hello."

"Are you Mrs. McKee?"

"Yes."

"Are you the Mrs. McKee who taught English at Central twenty years ago?"

"Yes, who is this?"

"It's Tom, Mrs. McKee, Tom Lowery!"

My mind went racing back to my first year of teaching in a small, rural school in Arkansas. I knew just who Tom was—that bright, freckle-faced red-head in freshman English class. I could still see him grinning from the second row.

"Tom, how are you, and how did you ever find me?"

I was floored! My first year to teach was not filled with memorable successes. With an art and history background, I wasn't exactly prepared for teaching high-school English. I spent my evenings keeping one step ahead of my students and begging help from "real" English teachers. To make matters worse, classes began in August, and we had no air conditioning. Morning classes were bad enough, but sweltering heat and gnats made afternoon classes nearly unbearable.

Hidden Potential

During the break at ten each morning, most of the boys went out to their privy (Yes, that's an outhouse!) and smoked. The girls had spent what little money they had on cancan petticoats and movie magazines instead of cigarettes, so they gathered at their privy to giggle over "secrets." All of this was culture shock to me. Oh, I'd been in privies, but they were not my favorite places, and I put off visiting them as long as possible. My neighbors soon learned not to speak to me as I rushed home from school until I had made a quick trip into the house.

My memories of those years were of hard work, primitive conditions, and students living near the poverty level. What memories could have prompted Tom to search me out and call after all this time?

"Oh, I just kept looking and asking. I can't believe I got you on the first call. Are you still teaching?"

I told him I was teaching fifth grade in a large open area. We had 4 teachers and 125 students in one room. "It's the newest thing in education, but I really miss walls between the classes. What are you doing now, Tom?"

I bit my tongue. I hoped I hadn't asked an embarrassing question. The students in his school had so little. After starting classes in early August, they had a two-week break in October, during which the children picked cotton to earn enough money to get through the winter. The school year ended in mid-April so the students could help pick strawberries. Many students fell asleep in class because they had been up all night catching chickens for shipment to the processing plant. Tom was the youngest of nine children, and his father worked in St. Louis to provide for their family. I couldn't imagine Tom leaving that little community, but how could he make a living there?

"Oh, I'm a pharmacist."

"A pharmacist! Why, Tom, that's great! Are you working for a drugstore?"

"Well, no, I'm working for myself. In fact, I own two pharmacies."

A gallon of milk nearly slipped out of my hand. I sank to the floor and leaned back against the cabinet as Tom told about his schooling and about the lives and successes of many of his classmates. His brother Jim was a high-school teacher. Two other brothers, Ben and Rob, became ophthalmologists, and some of his friends were now bank vice presidents and business executives. Obviously, while I was away teaching in Texas, the lives of my Arkansas students had changed more than I ever dreamed possible. One thing was sure, that grinning redhead had become more than a successful businessman. He had grown up to be an articulate, devout, and caring person. I was so proud of him!

"But, Tom, how did you manage to get the money for college?"

"Well, I got student loans and started at the junior college thirty miles away. Every Sunday afternoon I'd put on my sport coat, pick up my old suitcase, and go back to school for the week. Sometimes I had a ride, but many Sundays I hitchhiked to school. My family gave me five dollars to last the week. The cafeteria didn't serve meals on Sunday night, so I had to spend one dollar for supper. The other four had to last the rest of the week. After junior college, I went to the university to finish the three-year pharmacy program. It was hard sometimes, but I knew that my brothers had made it and I would too. Oh, I owed a lot of money when I got out, but I could make money with the degree. I just worked hard and paid off all my loans."

Finally, after forty-five minutes of updates and conversation, I asked the question that was burning a hole in my brain: "Tom, what do you remember about your freshman English class?"

"Oh, nothing specific," he said. "We just had a lot of fun, and you were always so excited about what you were teaching us. Oh yes, I do remember that one day you brought into class the first stereo record player we had ever seen. We heard sea gulls fly from one side of the room to the other, and we were amazed."

Whew! Tom's memories of the class were better than mine.

"Things really were tough," Tom said, "and not many graduates of our high school had been to college. But I guess we Lowery boys sort of led the way, and others began to follow."

"But, Tom, what gave you and your brothers the drive to do that?"

"My parents were not well educated themselves, but they valued education. And seeing my older brothers' success gave me hope. I never gave myself an out. I never even thought about quitting. No matter how long it took, I was determined not to leave until I had that degree."

Hidden Potential

It was satisfying to learn of Tom's inner strength and family support that I had known nothing about. I had hoped that somehow Tom, as well as the other students in that class, would find the necessary drive to go on past high school. Although I could see Tom's potential in that freshman English class, I did not see how it could be realized.

How refreshing it was to learn how the successful life of a past student had unfolded. The stories of Tom, his brothers, and his classmates encourage me greatly, not because of anything I did, but because of what it teaches me about our powerful God. I saw near-poverty and little hope for more, but God saw strength and success. The seeds of potential he had placed in Tom and the others exceeded even my imagination.

God of all wisdom,
Help me look beyond ragged jeans,
Gap-toothed smiles, and cowlicks
To see the grand potential you
Place within each child.
Show me how to nurture and encourage each
Budding seed to grow beyond my imagination—
To blossom beyond their dreams.

Recess

Slow down and remember why you became a teacher...

103

chapter seven

Revealed by Challenge

100 sheets • 200 pages
9³/₄ x 7¹/₂ in/24.7 x 19.0 cm
wide ruled • 09910

"Mrs. Flening is my favorite teacher because she is the science teacher. When I grow up I want to be just like her. Only I want more animals."

—Leia, age 10

drawing by Melinda, age 8

*D*ear Teacher,

Thank you for taking the time to talk to me in the hall the other day. You didn't know it, but what you said came at just the right time. I ended up not doing something that I now know would have been really stupid.

Thanks for the note you wrote in the margin of my paper fifteen years ago. I doubt you remember it, but I sure do. It stirred something in me. It lit a fuse that hasn't stopped burning. I'm a writer now. I hope that makes you proud. Enclosed is a copy of my first book.

Thanks for going to all the extra trouble with the visual aids. Most of my teachers just lecture. I learn better if I can see what you're talking about. I think I'm finally getting it.

Thanks for really being interested in the point I was trying to make in class last week. I think it's the first time a teacher has ever taken me seriously. It felt good.

Thanks for the personal challenge. I needed it.

Thanks for making school fun. The way you explain things, I don't even mind taking notes.

Thanks for showing up every day. You're the only one in my life who does.

Thanks for the field trip! Sure, it was great getting out of class, but some of the exhibits were really cool too.

Thanks for knowing my name.

Thanks for believing in me even when everybody else (including me) predicted failure. I don't know what you saw in me. You put up with a lot. Thanks for not giving up. Oh, and thanks for all the homework (just kidding!).

Love,
Your Students

Teacher, may the Lord repay you for what you have done. May you be richly rewarded by the Lord, under whose wings you have come to take refuge. Delight yourself in the Lord, and He will fulfill your heart's desires. Commit your ways to him and trust him, and he will do it. He'll help you shine!

Love,

Your God of Encouragement

Ruth 2:12;
Psalms 57:1; 37:4–6

Education is not to reform students or amuse them or to make them expert technicians. It is to unsettle their minds, widen their horizons, inflame their intellect, teach them to think straight, if possible.

—Robert M. Hutchins

Crossing Quicksand

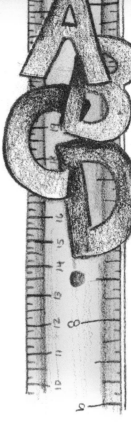

"Straighten up, Robert!"

"Get back in line, Robert!"

"Robert! Watch where you are going!"

Ann Brock's heart sank as she heard Robert being singled out. In the lunchroom, the teacher's aide loudly directed his every move, telling him where to sit, reminding him to push his chair in, and ordering him to pick up the milk carton that fell off his tray as he walked toward the trash can. This was Robert's life. He was treated as if his

113

absent-minded behavior and patient response to correction were signs of marginal ability. But Ann saw his special talents and, after much effort, finally got him admitted to the Talented and Gifted (TAG) program.

Nine-year-old Robert was big for his age and clumsy. He ambled around like a bear, bumping into everything that was between him and the place he wanted to be. When the TAG students lined up for class, Robert would invariably bump into the person at the end of the line, pushing at least three others off balance.

Group activities were a regular part of Ann's strategy to help Robert and the other students develop social and problem-solving skills. There was usually no rejoicing when Robert was assigned to a team. If the activity involved constructing something, they tried to keep Robert far away from the project—sure that he would crush it.

Today's activity was eliciting more complaints than usual. Their assignment was to get across a circle of "quicksand" using three boards, but only one at a time. "This one is impossible, Mrs. Brock! There is no way we can do this!" Robert's team had spent most of their solution-planning time on a plan that they now saw would not work.

Robert, who had been quietly tearing strips of paper, spoke up. "I think I know a way to do it." As usual, no one acknowledged his statement. The team continued to talk about several ideas but discarded them all.

Mrs. Brock announced, "You have two minutes to complete your plan."

"Oh no!" all the teams complained. "We're not ready!"

"I think I know a way to do it," Robert repeated.

"Well, we've got to do something. What's your idea?"

Robert used the strips of paper to explain his solution. When they argued that it wouldn't work, he reached into a game box and took out markers to represent each team member. Maneuvering the markers and strips of paper, he demonstrated the steps necessary to move the whole team across the space. When time was called, his team was still not convinced his plan would work, but having no other idea . . . they agreed to let Robert direct them.

As they watched each of the other teams fail,

they became even more convinced Robert's plan would fail too. They were the last team to attempt the crossing. Having no alternative, they followed Robert's instructions.

"Step here and move forward on the board. Good, now shift your weight to your left foot and hold the shoulder of the person on your left. Okay, now, reach out with your right foot but keep your weight on your left foot and scoot the next board forward." His directions were clear and spoken as if he were reading from a script. Occasionally, he paused to think, then he'd give the next set of instructions. They moved in slow motion, like a precision drill team with Robert monitoring every move.

Watching the team move across the "quicksand," the rest of the class saw a Robert they had never seen before. The goofy kid that everyone yelled at was really smart. "So that's why he's in our TAG class," Jenny whispered.

"Yeah!" several others agreed. Mrs. Brock saw Robert commanding the respect of his classmates for the first time in his life.

Crossing Quicksand

Robert calmly led the team off the last board and onto "solid ground." They had completed the crossing that no other team had been able to make. Shouting and jumping, Robert's team was joined by other classmates as they surrounded him and pounded him on the back.

As the teams formed a circle on the floor for the customary "debriefing," Robert whispered to Mrs. Brock, "Is this what happens when people like you?"

"Yes," she answered, "how does it feel?"

"Okay, I guess."

One of the students asked, "How did you remember all that?"

"I just looked in my mind."

Some of the other students nodded respectfully.

Not knowing how to respond to all the compliments, Robert spent most of the debriefing time looking at the floor. But when Ann saw a smile spread across his face, she had to swallow hard to keep her tears under control.

The team had crossed imaginary quicksand. Robert had crossed real quicksand, and his life was changed forever.

Revealed by Challenge

Abba, Father, show me how to
Challenge students to move
Into the fulfillment of the gifts
You have placed within them.

Recess

Put your feet up and recall the dreams you have for your students . . .

Look for these other *Hugs* books

Hugs for New Moms
Hugs for Daughters
Hugs for Girlfriends
Hugs for Women
Hugs for Teens
Hugs for Dad
Hugs for Friends
Hugs for Grads
Hugs for Kids
Hugs for Mom
Hugs for Sisters
Hugs for Grandparents
Hugs for the Holidays
Hugs for the Hurting
Hugs for Those in Love
Hugs for Grandma
Hugs to Encourage and Inspire
Hugs from Heaven: Celebrating Friendship
Hugs from Heaven: Embraced by the Savior
Hugs from Heaven: On Angel Wings
Hugs from Heaven: Portraits of a Woman's Faith
Hugs from Heaven: The Christmas Story